JR. GRAPHIC MONSTER STORIES

THE YETI !

STEVEN ROBERTS

PowerKiDS press

New York

Published in 2013 by The Rosen Publishing Group, Inc.
29 East 21st Street, New York, NY 10010

First Edition

Editor: Joanne Randolph
Book Design: Planman Technologies
Illustrations: Planman Technologies

Library of Congress Cataloging-in-Publication Data

Roberts, Steven, 1955-
 The yeti! / by Steven Roberts. — 1st ed.
   p. cm. — (Jr. graphic monster stories)
 Includes index.
 ISBN 978-1-4488-7905-2 (library binding) — ISBN 978-1-4488-8005-8 (pbk.) —
ISBN 978-1-4488-8011-9 (6-pack)
 1. Yeti—Juvenile literature. 1. Title.
 QL89.2.Y4R63 2013
 001.944—dc23
                        2012005786

Manufactured in the United States of America

CPSIA Compliance Information: Batch # SW12PK: For Further Information contact Rosen
Publishing, New York, New York at 1-800-237-9932

Contents

Main Characters

Charles Howard-Bury (1881–1963) British explorer who found footprints of a **yeti** in 1921 on an **expedition** in the **Himalayas**. His published **account** gained international attention.

John Jackson (1921–2005) Headed an expedition in 1954 to find evidence of the existence of the yeti. Recovered what he believed to be yeti hair from Pangboche **monastery** in the Himalayas.

Eric Shipton (1907–1997) British climber who came across strange footprints that he photographed while climbing **Mount Everest** in 1951. His photographs were later published.

N. A. Tombazi (c. 1920s) **Geologist** who, in 1925, saw a yeti in the Himalayas in Tibet.

Yeti Facts

- The yeti is thought to be **nocturnal** and an **omnivore**. High in the mountains, it may eat roots and berries. It may also catch and eat rabbits, mice, or even mountain goats.

- The yeti is said to walk with an upright **posture**, which means it stands like a person. Some say the yeti's foot has five toes. Its footprint may be as large as 13 inches (33 cm) wide by 18 inches (46 cm) long.

- The Himalayan people have many names for the yeti. They include *meh-teh* (man-bear), *mi-go* (wild man), and *kang-mi* (snowman).

The Yeti!

SAL, MARCUS, AND MARIA WERE CLIMBING IN THE MOUNTAINS WHEN A SNOWSTORM BEGAN TO MOVE IN.

THE HIKERS SET UP A CAMPSITE AND RADIOED FOR HELP.

HELLO, HELLO. IS ANYONE THERE?

THE HIKERS SETTLED IN AND WAITED TO BE RESCUED.

I HOPE RESCUERS GET TO US BEFORE A YETI DOES.

WHAT IS A YETI?

OH, IT IS JUST A STORY SOMEONE MADE UP.

IT'S NOT JUST A STORY, MARIA. LET ME TELL YOU SOMETHING. *THIS* IS YETI COUNTRY.

"THE YETI IS A **LEGENDARY** CREATURE THAT LIVES IN THE HIMALAYAS.

"THE HIMALAYAS ARE THE HIGHEST MOUNTAIN RANGE IN THE WORLD.

"PEOPLE OF THE HIMALAYAS HAVE WORSHIPPED THE YETI FOR CENTURIES AS A HUNTING GOD OR MOUNTAIN SPIRIT.

"ONE OF THE FIRST REPORTS OF A YETI TO REACH THE OUTSIDE WORLD WAS IN 1921. IT CAME FROM A CLIMBING EXPEDITION IN THE HIMALAYAS.

"CHARLES HOWARD-BURY LED THE EXPEDITION UP MOUNT EVEREST, THE WORLD'S TALLEST MOUNTAIN.

"THE CLIMBERS CAME ACROSS SOME VERY LARGE FOOTPRINTS."

STOP!

"HOWARD-BURY TRIED TO THINK OF SOME EXPLANATION FOR THE FOOTPRINTS."

PERHAPS SOME OTHER CLIMBERS CAME THROUGH HERE RECENTLY. OR MAYBE THE FOOTPRINTS ARE FROM A BEAR OR A WOLF.

"HIS SHERPA GUIDE QUICKLY CORRECTED HIM."

NO. THEY ARE FROM A WILD MAN OF THE SNOWS.

"HOWARD-BURY'S ACCOUNT APPEARED IN A NEWSPAPER.

E. G. LONDON TIMES

ABOMINABLE SNOWMAN

"A FEW YEARS LATER, IN 1925, A GEOLOGIST NAMED N. A. TOMBAZI WAS HIKING IN THE HIMALAYAS.

"TOMBAZI SPOTTED A FIGURE IN THE DISTANCE.

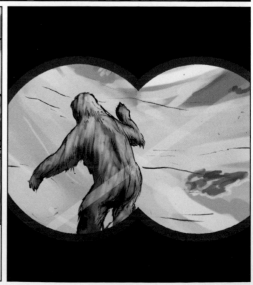

"HE TOOK A CLOSER LOOK AND WAS SURPRISED BY WHAT HE SAW. THE FIGURE WALKED UPRIGHT LIKE A MAN BUT WORE NO CLOTHES AND WAS COVERED IN FUR.

"MANY YEARS LATER, IN 1951, THE FAMOUS EXPLORER ERIC SHIPTON CAME ACROSS SOME STRANGE FOOTPRINTS WHILE SCALING MOUNT EVEREST.

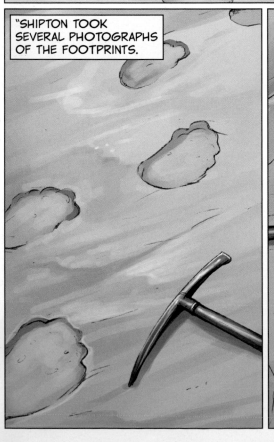

"SHIPTON TOOK SEVERAL PHOTOGRAPHS OF THE FOOTPRINTS.

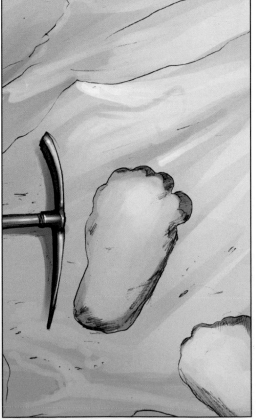

"THE PHOTOS WERE EXAMINED BY EXPERTS FROM AROUND THE WORLD."

I HAVE NEVER SEEN ANYTHING LIKE IT.

THIS WAS THE FIRST REAL EVIDENCE THAT THE YETI EXISTED.

WHAT HAPPENED THEN?

"THE BRITISH NEWSPAPER THE *DAILY MAIL* SENT A TEAM TO MOUNT EVEREST IN SEARCH OF THE YETI. THE TEAM WAS LED BY JOHN JACKSON.

"THE *DAILY MAIL* SEARCH TEAM FOUND A SET OF TRACKS THAT LOOKED LIKE THOSE OF A YETI.

"THEY SEARCHED IN VAIN FOR THE YETI. AFTER A TIME, THEY CAME UPON A **BUDDHIST** MONASTERY IN PANGBOCHE.

."INSIDE THE MONASTERY, THEY WERE SHOWN A PATCH OF FUR AND A HAND SAID TO BE THE REMAINS OF A YETI.

"ACCORDING TO LEGEND, THE FOUNDER OF THE MONASTERY WAS A **MONK** WHO LIVED IN A CAVE IN THE MOUNTAINS.

"THE WINTERS THERE WERE VERY HARSH.

"THE MONK SURVIVED BECAUSE OF THE HELP OF SOME FRIENDLY YETIS THAT BROUGHT HIM FOOD AND WATER.

"WHEN ONE OF THE YETIS DIED, THE MONK TOOK A PIECE OF ITS FUR TO PRESERVE ITS MEMORY."

GO IN PEACE, MY FRIEND.

"THE MONK BUILT THE MONASTERY TO DISPLAY THE FUR AND HONOR THE YETIS FOR THEIR KINDNESS.

"JOHN JACKSON WAS GIVEN A HAIR FROM THE PATCH OF YETI FUR TO TAKE WITH HIM.

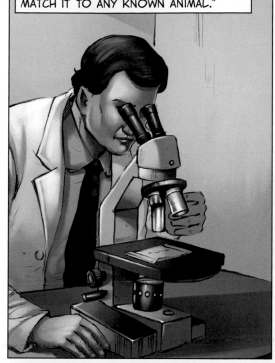

"THE HAIR WAS STUDIED BY SCIENTISTS AND COMPARED TO THE HAIR OF DIFFERENT ANIMALS. THEY COULD NOT MATCH IT TO ANY KNOWN ANIMAL."

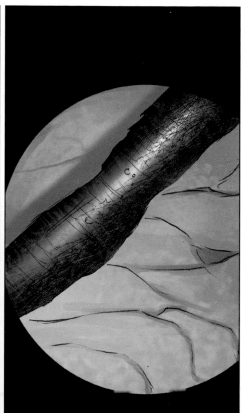

SINCE THAT TIME, THERE HAVE BEEN HUNDREDS OF YETI SIGHTINGS.

"SOME PEOPLE CLAIMED TO HAVE HAD A CLOSE ENCOUNTER WITH A YETI, BUT THEY COULD NOT PROVE IT."

WHAT IS THAT? I THINK IT'S A YETI!

"IN 1970, BRITISH MOUNTAIN CLIMBER DON WHILLANS REPORTED SEEING AN APELIKE CREATURE SEARCHING FOR FOOD NEAR HIS CAMP.

"IN 2007, THE AMERICAN TELEVISION SHOW *DESTINATION TRUTH* SENT A TEAM TO THE HIMALAYAS TO FIND PROOF OF A YETI.

"THEY DID NOT FIND A YETI BUT DID FIND A SET OF FOOTPRINTS AND MADE **PLASTER CASTS** OF THEM.

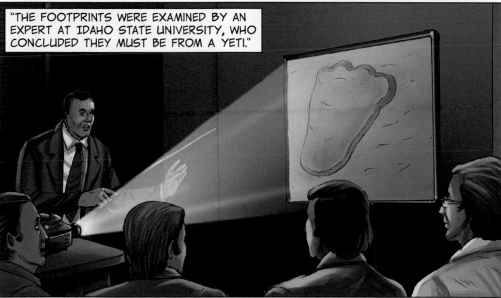

"THE FOOTPRINTS WERE EXAMINED BY AN EXPERT AT IDAHO STATE UNIVERSITY, WHO CONCLUDED THEY MUST BE FROM A YETI."

MANY PEOPLE ARE NOT CONVINCED THE YETI IS REAL, THOUGH.

"SOME EXPERTS THINK THE YETI IS A BEAR WHOSE FOOTPRINTS HAD MELTED IN THE SNOW SO THEY LOOKED BIGGER.

"OTHERS THINK IT COULD BE A *GIGANTOPITHECUS,* A CREATURE LONG THOUGHT TO BE EXTINCT.

"SOME PEOPLE THINK THE YETI MAY BE A WILD MAN WEARING ANIMAL FUR.

"OTHERS SAY THE STORIES ARE MADE UP. IN 1996, A TELEVISION CREW FILMED A YETI, WHICH THEY LATER ADMITTED WAS A HOAX."

GOOD TAKE!

"HOWEVER, REPORTS OF YETI SIGHTINGS CONTINUE TO COME IN FROM ALL OVER THE WORLD."

MARCUS FINISHED HIS STORY.

LAST WEEK, A YETI WAS SIGHTED ON MOUNT SHASTA, IN CALIFORNIA.

WHAT IS THAT?

SUDDENLY, MARCUS AND HIS FRIENDS HEARD SOMETHING OUTSIDE THEIR TENT.

A YETI!

More Yeti Stories

- **Slawomir Rawicz and the Yetis**
  In 1941, Slawomir Rawicz was captured and imprisoned by Soviet troops in his home country of Poland and later taken to Siberia. In his book entitled *The Long Walk*, Rawicz describes his escape from the Soviet prison camp and his walk through Tibet and the Himalayas to freedom. Rawicz claimed that high in the mountains he met a group of yetis. He described them as large, apelike creatures that walked on two legs.

- **Sir Edmund Hillary and the Yeti**
  In 1953, Sir Edmund Hillary and the Nepalese Sherpa Tenzing Norgay were the first climbers to reach the summit of Mount Everest. This made Sir Edmund Hillary world famous. In 1962, *National Geographic* published an article about Sir Edmund Hillary's search for the yeti in the Himalayas. His party found fur that it thought was from a yeti, but it turned out to be from a bear. Hillary attempted to prove that so-called yeti footprints could really be animal tracks that had just melted and become enlarged. After his investigations, Hillary became convinced that the yeti was just a legend.

- **Yeti Captured in Russia**
  In 2011, it was reported that Russian soldiers had caught a small female creature in the forest near Tashtagol, Siberia, that could not be identified. It was about 6 feet (2 m) tall, walked on two legs, and made strange grunting sounds. Its diet included both vegetables and meat. The Russians supposedly placed the animal in a zoo. People in Tashtagol reported that the captured female was just one of a group of yetis that lived in the area. They stole chickens and sheep from local farmers. A scientific expedition reported finding footprints and a place in a cave where the yetis lived. Many people later dismissed these stories as a hoax.

Glossary

account (uh-KOWNT) A story or description of events.

Buddhist (BOO-dist) Having to do with a religion founded in India.

expedition (ek-spuh-DIH-shun) A trip for a special purpose.

geologist (jee-AH-luh-jist) A scientist who studies the form of Earth.

Gigantopithecus (jay-gan-toh-pih-THEE-kus) An extinct ape that lived from one million to as recently as 300,000 years ago.

Himalayas (hih-muh-LAY-uz) A mountain range in Asia. It runs along the northern edge of Pakistan and India and the southern edge of Tibet and goes through Nepal and Bhutan.

legendary (LEH-jen-der-ee) Of or relating to a story, passed down through the years, that cannot be proved.

monastery (MAH-nuh-ster-ee) A house where people who have taken vows of faith live and work.

monk (MUNK) A man who has made certain promises based on his beliefs and who lives in a special house.

Mount Everest (MOWNT EH-vrest) The highest mountain in the world, located in the Himalayas on the border between Tibet, China, and Nepal.

nocturnal (nok-TUR-nul) Active during the night.

omnivore (OM-nih-vor) An animal that eats both plants and animals.

plaster casts (PLAS-ter KASTS) Shapes created in molds from a mixture of sand, water, and lime that hardens as it dries.

posture (POS-cher) The position of the body.

yeti (YEH-tee) A large, hairy creature that supposedly lives in remote mountainous areas, including the Himalayas.

Index

Websites

Due to the changing nature of Internet links, PowerKids Press has developed an online list of websites related to the subject of this book. This site is updated regularly. Please use this link to access the list:

www.powerkidslinks.com/mons/yeti/